# Dear Mr. President

Teen Voices
from Across the Country

Produced by the team at Write It Out Loud

Dear Mr. President: Teen Voices from Across the Country

Copyright © 2017
Ingrid Ricks

On behalf of Teens Across the Country

ISBN: : 978-0-9859294-5-9

All RIGHTS RESERVED

No part of this book may be reproduced in any form—electronic, mechanical, or with any other means, including photocopying—without the author's written permission, except in the case of brief quotations embodied in critical articles or reviews.

Cover Design by: Juli Saeger Russell

Interior Design by: Thea Chard

Published by: Write It Out Loud

www.writeitoutloud.org

# Table of Contents

| | |
|---|---|
| Our Intention with this Book | 5 |
| A Letter by Brea Fournier | 6 |
| *16, Cottonwood Heights, UT* | |
| A Poem by Miqueghele | 10 |
| *16, New Orleans, LA* | |
| A Letter by Elizabeth Chimalpopoca | 12 |
| *15, Los Angeles, CA* | |
| A Letter by Julia Tannenbaum | 16 |
| *16, West Hartford, CT* | |
| A Letter by Desean | 20 |
| *17, New Orleans, LA* | |
| Morning After Pill by Olivia Fryer | 22 |
| *17, West Jordan, UT* | |
| A Poem by Monty | 28 |
| *16, New Orleans, LA* | |
| Compassion by Sydney Janeway | 30 |
| *18, Seattle, WA* | |
| A Letter by Anna | 34 |
| *15, Los Angeles, CA* | |
| A Poem by Hannah Hurst | 38 |
| *17, Los Angeles, CA* | |
| A Letter by Antonio Martorano | 40 |
| *17, Seattle, WA* | |
| A Letter by Kevon | 44 |
| *17, New Orleans, LA* | |
| A Letter by Michael Raphael | 46 |
| *16, Los Angeles, CA* | |
| A Letter by Larah Helayne | 52 |
| *14, Mount Sterling, KY* | |
| Pride by Samantha Garcia | 56 |
| *16, Los Angeles, CA* | |
| A Poem by Ryan | 60 |
| *16, New Orleans, LA* | |
| A Letter by Brooke Taylor | 62 |
| *14, Austin, TX* | |
| Don't Lump Us Together by James McCreary | 68 |
| *13, New York City, NY* | |

| | |
|---|---|
| A LETTER by JOANNA SHEPHERD | 72 |
|     *15, Los Angeles, CA* | |
| A LETTER by JONATHAN | 76 |
|     *17, New Orleans, LA* | |
| TAKE IT TO THE STREETS! by MARLOWE BARRINGTON | 78 |
|     *15, Seattle, WA* | |
| A LETTER by MCKINLEY GOUGH | 84 |
|     *15, Taylorsville, UT* | |
| MELTING POT MOTHER TONGUE by JILLIAN JACKSON | 88 |
|     *15, Sammamish, WA* | |
| A LETTER by EMMA FRYER | 92 |
|     *17, West Jordan, UT* | |
| A LETTER by EMILY EDWARDS | 98 |
|     *Lee's Summit, MO* | |
| A LETTER by DESHAWN | 102 |
|     *17, New Orleans, LA* | |
| A LETTER by RILEY | 104 |
|     *15, Pittsburgh, PA* | |
| A POEM by REBECCA FIELDS | 110 |
|     *15, New York City, NY* | |
| A LETTER by CECE JANE | 114 |
|     *18, Los Angeles, CA* | |
| A LETTER by MARGARET ROSE MARIE HIGGINS | 118 |
|     *17, Edmonds, WA* | |
| A LETTER by SOPHIA GRUBER | 120 |
|     *16, West Hartford, CT* | |
| HEAR YE, HEAR YE by ERIN BLAKE | 124 |
|     *16, Salt Lake City, UT* | |
| LIVING IN FEAR by SIERRA WILSON-BAILEY | 128 |
|     *17, Los Angeles, CA* | |
| A LETTER by ANNIE BRAUN | 130 |
|     *12, New York City, NY* | |
| MY DREAM FOR AMERICA by KARA BATSON | 134 |
|     *17, Los Angeles, CA* | |
| A LETTER by KINSEY MAKKAR | 136 |
|     *16, Los Angeles, CA* | |
| SPEAKING OUT by SOPHIE DOWNING | 142 |
|     *17, Seattle WA* | |
| A MESSAGE FROM US by YEIN JI | 146 |
|     *17, North Salt Lake, UT* | |
| ACKNOWLEDGMENTS | 148 |

## Our Intention with this Book

So many teens around the country have experienced trauma and fear as a result of the recent presidential election, yet weren't able to have their voices heard at the ballot box because of their age.

"Dear Mr. President," a collection of letters, poems and essays from youth across the United States, is our effort to make their voices heard.

This anthology captures the serious concerns, hopes and dreams of teens from New York City to Los Angeles, Seattle to New Orleans. While the pieces cover a broad range of issues and fears, the overriding theme is one of hope and unity. It's about fostering love over hate, about inclusion vs. exclusion, about coming together to celebrate and ensure human rights for ALL—regardless of gender, race, religion, sexual orientation, citizenship, disability, health or economic status.

Today's youth are tomorrow's leaders. Thankfully, they have the wisdom and insight necessary to ensure that the United States and the world continue to thrive.

We urge you, President Trump, Vice President Pence and ALL Members of Congress to read this book, listen to the wisdom of our youth, and remember that we are only as great as our weakest link—and that diversity, compassion and acceptance are the principles on which the United States was founded.

# Brea Fournier

16
Cottonwood Heights, UT

Dear Mr. Trump,

Congratulations on your win.

I am not writing to defend you. I am not writing to enhance anger and desperation. I am writing to you because very shortly you are going to be President of the United States of America. As a U.S. citizen, I would like to discuss some of my concerns with you.

Mr. Trump, I am extremely passionate about human rights. I am only sixteen, but I plan to dedicate my life to this cause. It is no secret that many believe that you don't feel the same way. I however, think differently. I believe that deep down you are aware of what is right and wrong, and you know that every human is born with "unalienable rights." However, it is also no secret that your campaign has not carried that message.

I am asking you, with all my heart, for a few things.

Mr. Trump, at least while you are President, please remember it is your job to speak for minorities. Please defend their rights as much as you would defend your own. Remember that we are black, white, Latino, Muslim, Jewish, Christian, atheist, men, women, LGBTQ+...

And we are ALL American.

I'm asking you to remember that on the inside, we all look the same. And we all want a nation of peace. We have the right to the "pursuit to happiness" and we cannot pursue happiness whilst being turned against each other.

Allow your words to reflect a positive vision for this nation.

Wishing you the best,
Brea Fournier

# Miqueghele

## 16
## New Orleans, LA

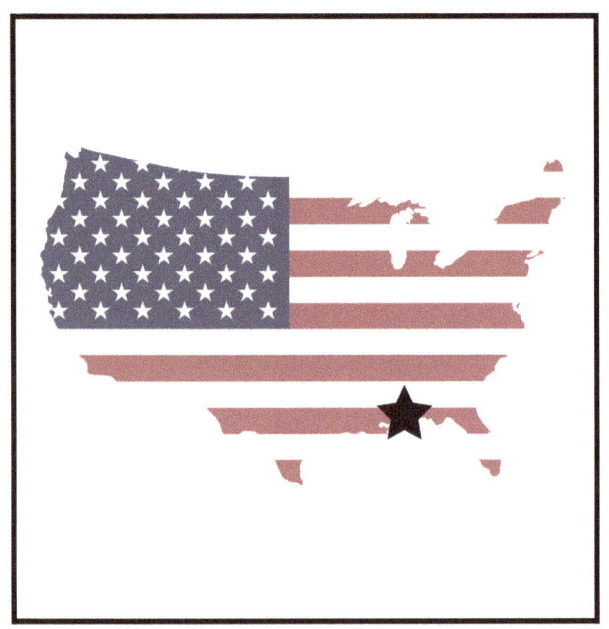

Dear Mr. President,

I hope my message is relevant.

Some people hear your name,

And imagine the States in pain,

But I think you can make a change.

We are all equal – blood runs through our veins.

I'm African American.

And I hope you don't find me strange.

# Elizabeth Chimalpopoca

### 15
Los Angeles, CA

Dear President Trump & Future Presidents,

America is or will be your nation, but it is a nation that you share with others: its citizens and its inhabitants. As their leader, you must take concern for them and do what is best for their wellbeing.

The United States of America is a multifarious nation that celebrates human rights, diversity, and inclusivity. Therefore, your term should not be beneficial for just one social group, one ethnic group, or any other group—but for all living in America. Regarding the matter of illegal immigration and deportation, there should not be any mass deportations for any ethnic group nor should a gigantic southern border wall be built to exclude people. Doing this would not do any good for America. On the contrary, it would conflict with the true American values, retrogress the progress America has made, and cause more social distress.

Mass deportations and building a wall will wreak havoc on families. No young boy nor young girl should have to suffer the pain of being separated from their parents and family members at a very young age, especially if it is for the sole reason that they are illegal immigrants without documents. Millions of young children and youth weep tears when their family members are forcibly taken away from them and deported to another country. Many more live in the constant daily fear that this could happen to them and are grateful at the day's end for having had their loved ones with them another day.

Unfortunately, I am one of those children who had to deal with this heartache. When I was only in the fourth grade and a young girl with a ponytail gleefully skipping out of my elementary school at 2:35p.m., blissful at the prospect of spending my afternoon with my mom and dad, I was told that my mother was getting deported.

That was when my life as I knew it started to fall apart. With my young innocence, I did not understand the full extent of this and I believed my mother would return to me soon. Sadly, this was not the case and I was left without a mother—a mother who wanted to be with me more than anything else in the world and who had not done anything wrong nor hurt anyone else.

My long year without my mom was a tumultuous one for me because I was put in the care of several family members and family friends in the hopes that they could step in as the important mother figure. I cried myself to sleep wishing my mom could come back and I was scarred for life. Luckily, my mom was able to come back to America. The day she came back I leapt into her arms and hugged her for what seemed like eternity. It was a day I will always cherish.

However, because of that experience, I now live in fear that she and I could be separated once more, even though there is no reason for it. This is a truth only a select few in my own life know, so please take note of the harm these sorts of actions take on actual human lives. This situation is something I do not wish for anybody else to go through, regardless of who they are and what they have done. Nor should it be something that others continue to agonize over today.

The only reason people from other nations come to this blessed nation we call the United States of America in the first place is to be safe, have better opportunities, and improve their quality of life. By permitting mass and unjust deportations, we would not only be failing them, but ourselves. These immigrants are good people. We, especially you in your position, have to take to heart everyone's interests and situations. You should not make deceptive generalizations of them to justify mass deportations and such actions. Presidents should not only be a figure of authority for their nation to look up to at times of trouble, but they should have a heart and genuinely care about their people's well-being, regardless of their citizenship. They should be realistically intelligent and wise.

I hope you take the words in my letter and my story, as well as those in many other letters you will receive, into consideration during your term, and that they influence you to take the correct executive action consciously.

Sincerely,
Elizabeth Chimalpopoca

# Julia Tannenbaum

## 16
### West Hartford, CT

Dear Mr. President,

On November 8th at eight o'clock in the evening, my two mothers, my younger brother, and I gathered around our TV, gleefully waiting for CNN to pronounce Hillary Clinton our first female president.

But it didn't happen.

I remember I started feeling ill around 10:30 p.m., after Florida finished counting votes. I couldn't believe it. You, a man who stands for everything my family is against, were going to be president instead. For the first time since the race began, I felt genuinely scared—like there was nothing I could do, nothing I could say, that would stop the inevitable adversity I feared we, devoted citizens of America, would face in the years to come.

I feared for myself and for other women that society has repeatedly deemed "lesser than" the favored male gender.

I feared for my mothers: two strong, independent gay women who, like every other LGBT family in our community, have fought so hard to gain the fundamental right to marry, a right that your own vice president threatens to abolish altogether.

I feared for my minority friends and for anyone else who has been discriminated against because their skin isn't white.

I feared for people with mental illness who are wrongfully mistreated due to the stigmas that deem us "crazy" and "insane." Mistreatment, I might add, police officers exhibit on a day-to-day basis.

And most of all, I feared for the future of my generation. We're too young to vote, to take part in determining who our younger siblings will look up to in the years to come. Like many children, when I was eight years old, I wanted to be president. Having so much fame, so much power, was an enthralling concept—or so it seemed at the time.

But just because I couldn't vote in this election doesn't mean my opinions are less important than those of someone older. Since December 15th of 1791 when Freedom of Speech was added to the Constitution, authorities have tried again and again to suppress the voices of juveniles, females, minority groups and anyone else looked down on in the eyes of our biased society with little success. Somehow, we've always found a way to be heard.

So hear me now, Mr. President, when I ask you to please, please don't take back all the progress we've made. We need you to build bridges, not walls. We need you to admonish anyone who insults others based on race, gender, religion, class, or sexual orientation. We need you to be a lover, not a hater, and to bring our divided nation closer together instead of pulling us further apart.

If you care about America, you will do these things. You will listen to the millions of voices vying for acceptance, equity, and love. You will listen, and you will act on it because regardless of your political standings, we are a democracy. We matter as well.

But if you don't, this isn't the last you'll hear from me, my family, and the countless other people who stood by Hillary Clinton to the bitter end. Know that we will not tolerate prejudice, nor will we abide by rules that prohibit us from living life to our full potential. Very few people have the capacity to become president but everyone—everyone—can make a difference simply by standing up for what they believe in.

America is already great, Mr. President. Now it's your turn to make it even greater.

Sincerely,
Julia Tannenbaum

# DESEAN

## 17
## New Orleans, LA

Dear Mr. President,

I have a question for you. What is your main goal? How will you make America great again?

There are two things I would like you to look into. The first thing is the public school education system. What can you do to help children's education in the future? The second thing is people living in poverty. What can you do to help low-income families and homeless people to have a decent life?

These are the main two situations we need to take action on. If you really want to make America great again, in my heart, and in my opinion, I think you should start there.

Desean

# Olivia Fryer

17
West Jordan, UT

## A Morning After Pill

Without a doubt this election year has been filled with many mixed emotions, late night rants, hope, and even progression.

Throughout the year, I heard all about how influential this election would be. At every turn of the radio dial, every click of the remote, there were news reporters and elected officials roaring rumors, fallacies, half-truths, and even the occasional fact. All of this made me feel attacked. However, this election year has helped me develop more of my own political and personal identity as a young woman, which is something I will forever value about this election season.

In the beginning I didn't know what to think of Trump's campaign. I looked at it like pretty much everyone else in the country: a joke. I had a constant inner dialogue telling myself he wouldn't make it past the debates, he wouldn't make it past the primaries, he certainly couldn't win the nomination. And then I told myself there was no way he could be president.

Everything was so surreal when he finally won the nomination. I didn't understand where all of these people on the right were coming from and why they were so angry at the entire country. I had been shut in my own little liberal bubble that is my performing arts school in Salt Lake City. Being stuck in my bubble was comforting at times, but dangerous when it came to facing reality.

November 8th was a genuinely positive day for me. I hand

painted t-shirts with "Nasty Woman" and "Herstory" in bright bold letters across the chest. I was proud and felt good when I wore it to school. I felt empowered knowing I would wake up the next morning and Hillary would be our president. However, when I returned home from my date on election night, I plopped down on the couch and immediately flipped on CNN to check the projections, I saw that Trump was up by about ten points. It was early so I wasn't terribly concerned. I figured when we moved on to the far east and California Hillary would surge ahead. But she didn't.

At around 1 a.m., while facetiming my boyfriend, tears streamed down my face, and I couldn't help but think it was all a weird nightmare. I knew even when I witnessed his blunt and terrifying acceptance speech that I would wake up and history would still be made.

The next morning I rubbed the sleep out of my eyes and rushed to flip on the news. It was plastered with nothing but talk about President-elect Trump. I was horrified. My dad had come downstairs to wake me up. He greeted me with, "Get up Livy, it's time to make America great again." I burst into tears once again, my eyes still puffy from the tears of the acceptance speech. After giving myself a blunt mental pep talk in order to prepare myself for not just the day ahead, but the next four years, I headed upstairs and threw on my nicest black clothing. It didn't seem appropriate to show up in anything else.

When I arrived at school, there was a stiff air of grieving around the school, like a student had just died. As I opened the doors, I was thrust into a sea of my peers with frowns and tears on their faces. They all lamented how terrified they were for their safety on the streets and also terrified that they would lose so much that they had worked for over the past eight years.

My school, filled with almost every minority imaginable, was in mourning. The feeling of some sort of warped reality filled every crevice in my little high school. An image of some sort of a "national morning after pill" filled my mind. Some kind of takesy backsies spell to cast on the whole system. All day I found myself overcome with thinking of ways to prevent this upcoming administration from occurring.

The feelings I felt throughout that day at school were simply unforgettable. I'd never felt something so incredibly powerful. Time seemed to stop, as if we were all moving through amber. It was a touching sense of community you would never imagine in a high school setting. That day was filled with tearful hugs, little crooked smiles to each other across the hallway, looks that would simply tell you, "Hey, I love you, and we're gonna get through this together." How was I supposed to leave this environment? This place where I felt so incredibly safe, loved, and like I could change things—really change things.

I'm still figuring out how to use those feelings to effect real political change and to decide what the best thing I can do for my community is. I don't know what the future holds, but know that

I have at least some power to make changes. That I have a family that supports and takes pride in my political passion is extremely encouraging.

# Monty

## 16
## New Orleans, LA

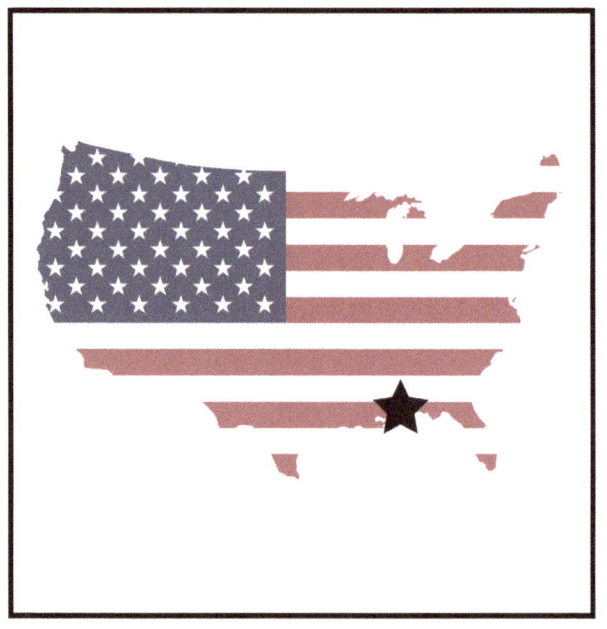

Dear Donald Trump,

Man to man, colored to non-colored, I'm reaching out to you as a voice of the average urban minority.

You may call it ghetto, but we call it survival. Since the days of slavery, all it's been about for people labeled "other" is survival. I'm currently in jail for reasons I do not wish to further explain. It's nothing capital though. Does that make you look at me differently?

If that shapes your image of me, and if you put me into a statistic, read no further. But if you are with me and have concern, continue to read.

And this is where I start. Since America became America, it was known as "the land of the free," but it wasn't free for Native Americans, and it wasn't free for Africans who were forced to come to America. Why would the "Founding Fathers" mislabel the country like that?

I don't like to dwell on the past because it's traumatizing. I just don't want the past to come back to haunt me. Now people say you're no good, or you're unfit for the presidential position, and I can't comment because I don't know you. But I have faith in God that He will lead you to make the right decisions.

-IOL CEO
Monty

# Sydney Janeway

18
Seattle, WA

## Compassion

Dear Mr. President,

It is fear that keeps me up at night; fear of how we will tackle something so daunting as global warming when we can't seem to stop killing each other for one moment.

There's police brutality, corporations controlling our government, systemic racism, and a wealth gap increasing by the second. We have groups terrorizing entire hemispheres and women still being denied basic human rights, but all of these issues would be resolved if people had a bit of compassion for one another. This is a social obligation we have always had for each other, yet we continue to fall short.

We have to start seeing each other as people, with moms, dads, sisters, brothers, loves, and children, rather than police-killers, terrorists, racists, sexists, bums, conservatives or communists. Only then will we make progress in this world. When we start focusing on what unites rather than what divides us, compromise will follow. Only through compromise can we start to battle global issues such as climate change.

With such a broad answer, how can someone like me do anything about it? I see everyone as a line of dominoes, with me at the start. When I continuously send joy, support and understanding to everyone who surrounds me, many will in turn do the same. It's having a genuine interest in the well-being of the people around you, even those you've never met. That can be asking about their day, being there for people to lean on, or simply, smiling at every person you pass.

I know if everyone just started to realize we are equals and all in this together, issues would resolve, our problems would begin to fade and there'd be nothing standing between me and my much-needed sleep.

Mr. President—will you help lead the way?

Sydney Janeway

# Anna

**15**
Los Angeles, CA

Dear Future Presidents of the United States,

My name is Anna and I am fifteen years of age. Although I am young, I have seen the ways of humanity: the decisions they make, the words they let loose from their mouths, the lives they live, and most importantly, the evil they are capable of.

With the ultimate power of free will to say and do what we please, several people are drawn to paths of destruction leading to the continuation of the downfall of mankind. Constantly, I see people around me giving in to the darkness and evil within them; people taking the lives of others, people cheating on and divorcing their spouses, people hating their fellow man, and the list goes on.

I have seen leaders, such as presidents, that have failed to steer our country as a whole and instead divided people. As president, your job is to lead us, be an example for us, unite us, provide us with hope, change people's lives for the better, be devoted, be honest, promote equality amongst all, and not just declare our future will be successful, but make our future successful.

Giving our nation hope is one of the most difficult jobs to accomplish. Although you cannot change everyone's life, you can reveal to them a true source of hope. You yourself cannot be the true source of hope, but you can experience this hope and exude it throughout the nation. We look to you and expect great things. But you are just a human being; you cannot do this by yourself.

"What is this hope?" you might be asking. Just look to the

dollar bill, recite the Pledge of Allegiance, and/or read the Declaration of Independence! All these things have one specific thing in common: God. God is such an important part of our lives today and believe it or not, He is the ruler and leader above all.

In Psalm 67, it says, "May God be gracious to us and bless us and make his face shine on us—so that your ways may be known on earth, your salvation among all nations. May the peoples praise you, God; may all the peoples praise you. May the nations be glad and sing for joy, for you rule the peoples with equity and guide the nations of the earth. May the peoples praise you, God; may all the peoples praise you. The land yields its harvest; God, our God, blesses us. May God bless us still, so that all the ends of the earth will fear him."

Think about this passage and see that the secret to a successful presidency is revealed here!

Know that if you are going to lead my country, I am trusting you to look to the example that God has set for all of us. Abide by His rules and act as He does, truthfully and loyally, leading not only every nation, but all our hearts as well. God loves all of us and is not just an example for us, he is our friend and gives our lives meaning!

So, fellow presidents, I honor you and the stand you have taken to lead our country into success but truly I tell you: love God, follow God, honor Him, obey Him, listen to Him, serve Him, and learn from Him. For God will teach you to lead as He does and for your people, for me, for the Lord your God, remember, "In everything you do, put God first, and he will direct you and crown your efforts with success." There lies our hope.

Sincerely,
Anna

# Hannah Hurst

17
Los Angeles, CA

The streets and the beach of LA
is where I love to stay.
The cool breeze
and the summer tease
feels like home,
no matter where.

Going into this election
with all the selections
I was worried about feeling at home.
I may be a democrat,
but that doesn't mean I won't let
Trump have a crack at it.

My home, most importantly has equality,
or at least some of the discrimination has been put on mute.
I'd like to keep it that way.

The closer and closer we got to the election
I fell into a daze…
Panting… and fainting…
But in the end it will all be OK
Because I know God made it this way.
If God has faith in Trump, then so do I.

# Antonio Martorano

**17**
Seattle, WA

Dear Mr. Trump,

I am a white, seventeen-year-old libertarian-leaning liberal male. I grew up in an upper-middle class neighborhood just north of Seattle, Washington.

Growing up in the Northwest has been an incredible experience. In my seventeen years of living in this state, I've had the spectacular opportunity to experience the superfluity of environments; from the raging coasts of Cape Flattery, to the desolate prairies of the Colville Reservation, and everything in between. The natural environment has become a place special to my heart, the tranquility it offers, the endlessness it supplies, and the memories it produces is un-equatable to anything else I can imagine in my life.

When something I love is endangered, it's up me to question whether or not it's worth it to try to save it. It's no secret that our world is suffering. Our climate is changing. Our oceans are rising and becoming more acidic. Our glaciers and ice sheets are retreating, and hundreds of species become extinct every day. I may not see such distinguished effects like these in my everyday life, but all one has to do is look at the facts to see the proof.

For fifteen years, I hadn't experienced much more than what the United States had to offer when it came to nature. I had already seen sights like the Grand Canyon and Niagara Falls, walked the windy beaches of Duluth, and plunged into the depths of Catalina Island. Yet, I still felt deprived from what the rest of the world had to offer. I felt isolated from other cultures. I felt as if all my travel up to this point had been comfortable; I knew that the only way I could experience other cultures was to expose myself to the rest of the world. So, in a swift exchange of conversation with my parents, I signed up to be a member of the National Geographic Student Expedition to Brazil in the summer of 2014.

Looking back on that trip, it's hard to imagine some of the things we did. I remember walking in the Amazon rainforest, feeling sudden sharp pains on my thigh, only to later find out that I had literal ants in my pants. I have vivid memories of waking up at 5 a.m., sweating because of the 90 degree, 100 percent humidity conditions, unable to fall back asleep. I can remember eating the same type of food everyday: grilled meat, Brazilian rice, beans, and a seemingly endless supply of watermelon. Yet, looking back, all of these supposedly negative events culminate together as part of the experience as a whole; and therefore, are positive to my growth and development as a citizen of the Earth. It was that experience that changed my view of the world. It was that experience that opened my eyes to the true danger of climate change.

Unfortunately though, I look to your presidency and question your understanding of what we have here on Earth, and its preciousness. Our existence as a species is a miracle in the greatest regards to space and time. We only have one Earth, and it's up to us to keep it as healthy as possible. I understand that it's difficult to change our perspective on the world, and sometimes it takes an experience to do so. But I urge you to consider the fact that not only do we share this Earth with millions of other species, we share this Earth with the future generations of humans that have yet to experience life.

So, I urge you, Mr. President, to take a step back, and realize that your self interests, and even the self interests of the citizens of the United States, aren't in line with the interests of global health. I urge you to question the value of a barrel of oil over the life of a newborn child. We as a species need to realize that the later we act on this issue, the chances of us surviving will continue to decrease. And although it may not happen in your lifetime, or even my lifetime, it will happen in someone else's lifetime. And they will be the generation to suffer because of our blatant negligence to our own actions.

It's time to finally hold ourselves accountable. It's time for change.

Antonio Martorano

# KEVON

17
New Orleans, LA

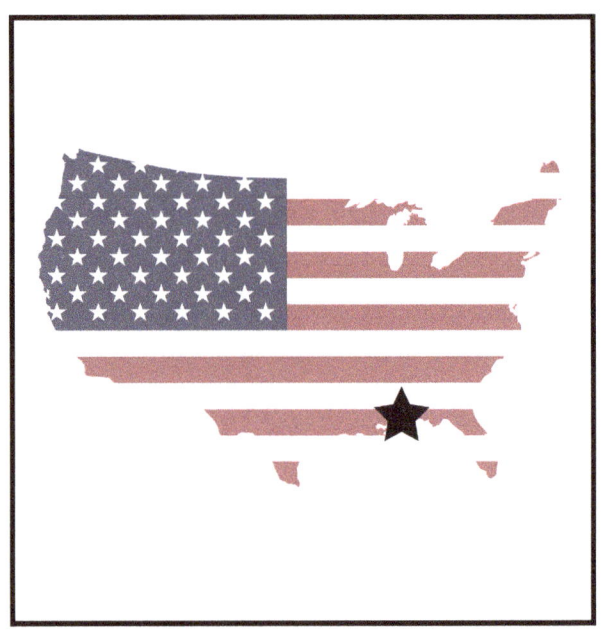

Dear Mr. President,

I don't think it's fair that you are trying to take away Muslim freedom. I think that every religion should have the right to live wherever they want.

You say that you're going to make America great again, but you're taking away our loved ones. That's not the way to fix the economy. All races and religions should be welcome in the United States.

Kevon

## MICHAEL RAPHAEL

16
Los Angeles, CA

Dear President Trump and future Presidents of the United States of America,

I would like to share my thoughts with you on how the 2016 election's circumstances originated, progressed and concluded, along with the current state of our nation and what this means for the future of America and the world.

Before I begin, I need to share a disclaimer: I did not overwhelmingly favor you or any other candidate in this election, and I say this because I want to provide thoughts based on what I've experienced observing the election, governed by what I think, and not so much as to what I feel; however, I will reserve my requests for the end. Let's begin.

The results on November 8th were no doubt unprecedented by a majority of the nation as illustrated in popular vote, but to a much larger scale since voter turnout was around 58 percent—meaning that around 90 million eligible voters didn't vote. But putting this aside, what really matters is why your message resounded with so many Americans and how you became a presidential candidate in the first place. To do this, we must turn to history and analyze how it managed to repeat itself.

While there have been many right-wing politicians around the world elected to office based on aspects such as nationalism, xenophobia, racism, etc., notable examples can be found in the early 20th century with figures such as Benito Mussolini and Adolf Hitler. Those fascist parties rose to power not just based on the aforementioned reasons, but also because of the poor economic status of their countries, which fell victim to the stock market crash of 1929 and by receiving the short end of the stick following World War I.

From this, we can ascertain a trend: a weakened economy and decaying national image combined with prejudice-induced demagoguery, if successful, leads to mass popularity and subsequently a sharing of the candidates' ideals. From this, the blame-game starts, pinning responsibility for the nation's current state on the establishment and the incumbent party. History repeated itself right in front of our eyes, with the parallel being the stock market crash of 1929 resurfacing in an altered manifestation almost a century later in the stock market crash of 2008. This created the necessary environment for frustration to build. Although efforts were made to ease it in the past eight years, the damage had already been done and the stage was set for someone separated from the status quo. But enough about history, let's now focus on the nature of the campaign as it progressed.

It's an understatement to say that the campaign was an unorthodox (and expensive!) one. The people's anxieties and frustrations combined with the polarization of the political spectrum resulted in an equally divisive campaign trail, which in turn, used tactics to divide the nation left or right. Many insults and accusations were thrown from both sides of the aisle, but I guess you saw these tactics simply as means to an end, following the infamous Machiavellian principles.

Whether or not you actually meant all the things that you've said, which I need not mention, it by all means raised some eyebrows. But some have seen through this aggressive facade that you've put up and voted for you, including even some Muslim women who ignored your outspoken comments and policies geared against Muslim-Americans. And you used the same tactics to blast your Republican and Democratic opponents out of the water, especially with Jeb Bush. These tactics worked because it was their established names at stake, and frankly, you had nothing to lose. If you lost, you could still go back to your billion-dollar empire, whereas for them, they'd be stuck with their previous positions and popularity, and not the presidency.

So now we've covered why you won and how you won, which basically summed up is that the economic situation of the country and the dissatisfaction from the status quo incumbent party created a near-perfect environment for you to campaign in. And you utilized this situation to win over your audience and eliminated your opponents by means of aggressive tactics that tarnished your opponents' reputations, and a lot of times by the well-known logical fallacy: ad hominem. But now let's talk about what I expect from you.

Frankly, I expect that you fulfill the promises you made to the American people to better the state of this nation, and as you do that, I expect you to not have a do-it-all-by-myself attitude, because no one can fix this nation alone. I request for you to utilize all the resources you have available and to be able to compromise frequently in order to work towards the bigger picture of bettering America.

And speaking of compromise, I would like you to invest in renewable energy, because this nation can't run on fossil fuels healthily forever. Also, I would like you to work on lowering crime and improving infrastructure, which includes the areas of education, inner cities, and for hospitals as well. The next one I am about to mention may be the hardest: improve relations with minorities that have been alienated as a result of the campaign. In order for this nation to come one step closer to embracing their new president, the least you could do is try to make amends.

Lastly, if you're going to build the wall, do it in such a way that won't cost taxpayers a ridiculous amount of money. I know this sounded like a critique at times, but this was about as objective as I could be. Thank you for your time.

Sincerely,
Michael Raphael

## Larah Helayne

### 14
### Mount Sterling, KY

Donald Trump,

You should know that the thought of you running this country has terrified me from the very beginning. When I discovered that this was my new reality, my heart shattered in fear, too afraid to keep beating.

As easy as it would be to hate you for the hate you've spread; I have chosen to move forward in love. Here are some things you should know.

I am a broke, 14-year-old orphan who relies on the government for every one of my basic needs. I live with my grandmother, who is on disability, and my grandfather, who is recently retired.

We get by. I am blessed to have always had enough, but without the help of the government, my life would be a different story. I receive Social Security every month, and I am currently in distress because Matt Bevin has cut the program from which I received health insurance.

No teenager—no human—should end up in tears because they don't know if they'll be able to afford basic health care. I don't want anyone to have to go through that, because honestly, it's terrifying,and unfair.

The experience of losing my parents and having to seek government assistance financially has opened my eyes to how important programs like Welfare, Social Security, and Obamacare are. Please protect these programs. Remember people like me, who could very well end up in extreme poverty without them.

    Mr. Trump, I am also a woman. A proud, bisexual feminist, who has spent my entire life fighting to be heard. Fighting for my body to be my own—not a victim to testosterone—screaming over catcalls and microaggressions, only to be told that I am not worthy of the breath within my lungs. Hiding myself, and pushing hands away, and still being blamed for the men who think it's alright to "grab us by the pussy."

    You, thus far, have only ever added to my problems, with your careless misogyny, homophobia, and disregard of minorities.

    I hope you have learned that it's not okay to touch a woman without consent, to touch anyone without consent, and it's certainly not okay to promote such behavior.

    I hope you know that LGBTQ+ youth are already four times more likely to kill themselves than straight people, and that taking our rights away would certainly not help the matter.

    I hope you understand that this is a country built by immigrants, who wanted nothing more than a better, freer life.

    You should know that my Hispanic, Muslim, immigrant friends, are much better Americans than you will ever be. They uphold love, unity and freedom in a way that I doubt you could even comprehend, and sending them away from this country would only leave more room for darkness to grow.

    People seem to think that you condone hate, and I pray that's not true. I have received more homophobic remarks since you've been elected than all the days before that combined. I have been told more than ever, that as a woman, my job is simply to please men, to "stay in the kitchen where I belong" and "make them a sandwich."

It's almost as if, because the president-elect has said some disgusting things, it makes it okay for the rest of the country to do the same.

Stop being silent about this. Speak up and stop turning your head away from hate crimes committed in your name.

Mr. Trump, if nothing else, I ask this: that you would keep your hate and intolerance to yourself. It is hard enough to live in this world, as a woman, or a person of color, or a member of the LGBTQ+ Community. It is already hard enough to accept and love oneself.

Please don't make these things impossible.

Remember that now, when you speak, all the world is listening. Every action, every word, matters. Make these next four years count, and for the love of progress, don't take any steps backward.

Don't you think for a second that we, the diverse America, won't put up a fight. We will not let you take away our rights. We will not let you stifle our voices. We will be loud, and proud, and make ourselves heard. You cannot drown out the sound of freedom.

Larah Helayne

# Samantha Garcia

16
Los Angeles, CA

## Pride

Even though the time that Eliana and Becky had together was transient, it was also special. Never before had Eliana felt so close to someone. Eliana kissed Becky one last time before she would leave her forever. The warmth of their last kiss permeated throughout Eliana. They wanted to come out soon. Well, they were going to come out after Hillary Clinton won the presidency, but that was all in the past now. How could they come out to a nation full of hate led by a leader who thought that they were bound for hell?

Tears streamed down both of their faces because they now knew that they could never be together. They felt as if they had a fetter around them. Eliana desperately wanted to hold Becky's hand in public without being scourged. It was like a modern tale of Romeo and Juliet, except it was not two cities that was keeping them apart, it was their country. They sat together one last time. Eliana memorized every detail of Becky's face. People were threatened by them because they were not just another archetype of their society. They felt unwanted and betrayed by the country that they once had loved.

They knew that their feelings for each other seemed heinous to others. But, to them, it was perfect, and there was nothing more right than anything else that they had ever felt with another person before. Eliana and Becky had been suppressing their feelings towards women for a long time now because they were ashamed of what they felt, but now that they finally accepted who they really were everything became clear. It was like receiving glasses after years of being blind, and now they could finally see. The Star-Spangled Banner meant nothing now. What was the point of living? What was the point of doing anything? For the next four, or maybe eight, years she would feel trapped in a stuffy closet.

Eliana couldn't talk to anyone about her relationship with Becky or even her feelings about the election because even her parents had voted for the bastard. She could not accept God right now either. She resented him because he let this happen. He let people hate her. There was not much to do now, so she decided to run. Eliana could not just wheedle her way through life anymore. She didn't know where she would go, but at least it would be better than this place.

# RYAN

### 16
### New Orleans, LA

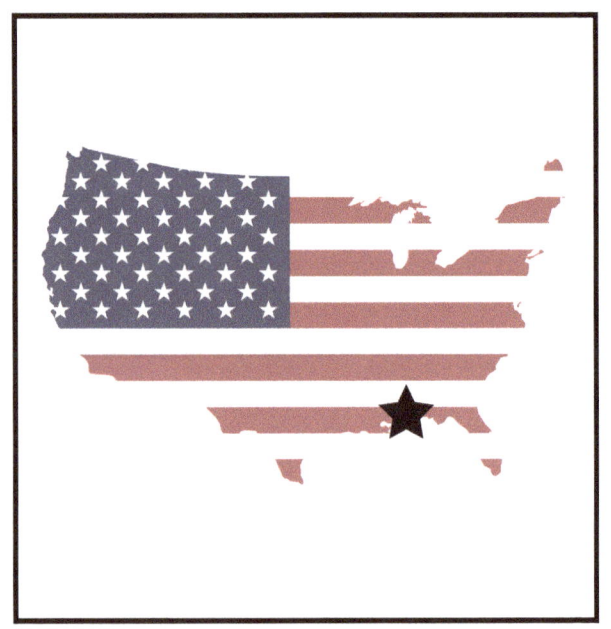

Dear Mr. Trump,

You're going to be a pain in the brain,
You know, in small cities
Like New Orleans –
We have a lot of economic crimes, money crimes
Because our people can't find decent jobs
They think they have no other way
To support their families.

It seems to me that,
The United States are all about money
And for those of us who have none,
We have no place here.
Don't be greedy.
Please help us come together.
Please help make get better.

Ryan

# BROOKE TAYLOR

14
Austin, TX

Dear Mr. President,

What defines someone as American? Which characteristics and qualities do you have to possess in order for you to truly label yourself as an American? I'm not talking about the legal documents or borders, the physical aspects that seem to dictate a person's nationality. I'm talking about the common and obvious morals, values, and interests all loyal Americans possess.

Before the election, I thought all of America was a united front, fighting together to make sure everyone, regardless of what they looked like or what their heritage is, got the right to life, liberty, and the pursuit of happiness. If you had asked me these questions years ago, I would have told being an American meant that you were accepting, loyal, hard-working, and free.

Perhaps it was just childhood ignorance, or perhaps it was just the changing of times. Either way, no longer do I share that belief. No longer do I believe that all of America stands together, fighting for each other. No longer do I believe that in order for me to make it in this world, all I have to do is work hard. What has lead me to adopt this pessimistic attitude towards my country and future in such a short amount of time, you may ask? Well to that my answer is simple. And that is the Election of 2016.

Growing up, I always remember my parents and teachers telling me to always be kind and play nice with the other kids, no exceptions. As a kid, no exceptions to me always meant no exceptions. It did not mean that I have to play nice and share my toys with everyone, except for Gabriel because his parents are Mexican. It did not mean I could steal Maya's toys because she's Muslim. That would be a preposterous thing to teach a child, right? Then why is most of government and society functioning like this? Why do we say that all men are created equal, when black males are 5.1 more times likely to be incarcerated that their white counterparts? Why do we say that every person has the right to the freedom of religion, yet we are banning an entire religion from entering our country? It seems that our government is run on exceptions.

So, what does all of this have to do with the Election of 2016? For me personally, I felt like the whole election was a huge exception. Like I said, before then I had felt like every American shared the same values and morals. I believed that while our nation still did have many disputes and conflicts, we at least could agree on some principles and some topics, for example, the simple and apparently not-so-common opinion that misogyny and racism were wrong. I would never have believed anyone, or at least very few people, would ever vote for someone who was point blank racist/sexist. But exceptions were made when it came to Donald Trump.

I was always quite baffled by each excuse the American public made for our now President. I don't see how mocking a disabled reporter or having twelve women accuse him of sexual assault wasn't the end of his entire campaign. Nonetheless, it wasn't the end, and now we're all left to pick up the pieces and try to figure out what went wrong.

While I want to believe that the reason Trump won was due to the lack of education of the effectiveness of his plans as president or the lack of awareness of some of Trump's comments towards women and other minorities, I also have to face the reality of this situation. This election reflects on the ideals and morals of the citizens of America, which are no longer unified. And that is what scares me the most.

Right now, at this very moment, all I can say in regards to the future of our nation is that I'm scared. The fear that was promoted, promised and used to win the Election of 2016 is now going to be at the heart of our government and society. As a girl, I am scared for my safety and prosperity. As a friend to many people of different ethnic backgrounds, I am scared for their safety and their basic human rights.

Through this entire election, me and much of my generation have felt silenced and ignored. No one gave us much thought when they placed their ballots. But we are the future of America. We are the ones who are going to be carrying out your legacy and your parent's legacy. Do not leave us in chaos. Do not leave us with a divided nation that can't even remember the basic structure and fundamentals it was built upon.

Mr. President, I urge you to be strong leader. I urge you to be the best leader this nation has ever seen. I do not want to see my home split in two, fighting each other. But you must take into account every single citizen of this great nation. Do not ignore the worker at the gas station, or the person cooking your food. They are the backbone of America, they represent the millions of people who work hard every day and pay their fair share of dues to live in this country. Represent those people, not just the top 1 percent. Represent those of every single skin tone and religion, for we mustn't forget that America is built upon immigrants and those who come here looking for a better way of life. Represent all Americans, for that is your job Mr. President, no exceptions. So please, help us in picking up the shattered pieces of our nation.

Brooke Taylor

# James McCreary

**13**
New York City, NY

## Don't Lump Us Together

Has anyone ever judged you based on one trait that you have? Has someone ever called you a mean name, without even bothering to ask you who you are?

That is wrong. No one should ever assume anything about you without fully knowing you. This is why I was so shocked when I watched a YouTube video featuring a violent, radical activist. I watched the video without agreeing or disagreeing. Then the woman opened her mouth, and said a few small sentences that nearly caused me to burst into tears.

She claimed "our society ensures that all whites are racist, and all men are sexist, because they benefit from the system of power."

I was outraged. How could someone say that I was racist or sexist, without even knowing me, or knowing that there are many different people in my family of different races, or that it is also heavily dominated by women?

Growing up, it was common for people to get angry with me for things that other people like me have done, especially when learning about civil rights in school. At one point, a few years ago, an African American man got angry at my dear nanny, who is from Trinidad, for being seen in public with a Caucasian boy. He didn't even know how important this woman was to me, having been there the day I was born. Now, a few months after my mother passed, she is one of the biggest comforts in my life.

It pains me to think that there are people still out there like this woman and this man—people who would assume that I am racist and sexist without even knowing that I am half Jewish, and also part Asian by marriage. Or without knowing that I am a political activist who tries to help my family and anyone else in need.

Some people feel the need to throw me under the bus for things that people similar to me have done, without knowing that I go out of my way to help all races and sexes. It is unjust and wicked to call anyone a word like "racist," "sexist," "mean," or "evil" without even knowing who they are.

If you dig a little deeper into yourself or others, you'll find facts you never knew. After thinking about myself, I recalled diversity groups that students from my school were attending a few months ago. One of these groups, which was for white males, was called "Re-establishing Power." Upon hearing this name, my initial reaction was to claim that this group was a horrible, racist idea. But after a while, I realized what this name really meant. It was about trying to use your powerful voice to help and support others.

As someone who prides myself most on being a kind and sweet person, I was shocked when the footage of President-Elect Trump was released. His comments about women promoted an even worse impression of men in general. But when Michelle Obama made her speech at a campaign rally for Hillary Clinton, I was truly inspired. Her words made my heart glow, and helped prove that not all men are sexist. This beautiful speech inspired me to try to convince everyone I knew to vote for Hillary Clinton. She is a smart, talented woman who, I feel, really wanted to be the first woman president, and now won't. It was a huge loss and I am devastated.

Now there is all the more reason for people to call me racist or sexist.

I know moving to Canada has become a joke by now, but when Trump was first elected, it seemed like the best choice I could make. I still wish to live in a land where no one will judge me based on anyone else's actions. I hope that Hillary Clinton or Michelle Obama will become the next president to stop this man from eliminating the American Dream for everyone. The wall, as well as Mr. Trump's harsh views on social issues, are truly a concern to me.

I hope that one day the American Flag will truly be able to fly over the Land of the Free and the Home of the Brave.

# JOANNA SHEPHERD

### 15
### Los Angeles, CA

Dear Mr. President,

On the evening of October 4, 2016, my kitchen was crowded by a throng of family members, each wearing a certain, troubled frown, squinting and craning their necks towards our television screen in an attempt to follow the incoherent cacophony of belligerent vice-presidential candidates bickering.

I leaned against the olive-colored couch my siblings were sprawled upon, next to my mother who had abandoned the vigorous scrubbing of a grease-stained frying pan to try and make out what the politicians were saying. The moderator waved her arms in exasperation, but any objections to the chaos were drowned out by the two men whose debate had altogether given way to contemptuous shouting.

The remainder of the vice-presidential debate followed in similar fashion, heavily peppered by interruptions, sarcasm, and condescension. I was appalled. Not only was it rude, but it was difficult to understand what either were even saying.

I wanted to scream, "Just stop already! Can't you see that someone else is speaking? Why are you interrupting when you're supposed to be listening?"

Now more than ever, it is crucial for those who have been given megaphones to refer to standard human decency. Remember that there are always going to be people watching, and on national television, how you act toward each other at the podium sets the standard for how the people on the home front treat others with whom they disagree. What sort of message do you think that you are broadcasting when you roll your eyes and shake your head mockingly?

What I'm trying to say is, as a political figure, you have social responsibilities. Right now, our country is in pain. Family members, friends, classmates, and complete strangers on the Internet are lashing out at each other, spitting names: hateful, intolerant, narrow-minded. But aren't we all on the same team? Everyone believes that they are on the right side of the fight. But instead of raising our voices, hurling insults, and interrupting, what would happen if we could all just listen a little more closely? To reassure the middle school student who is learning US History that this really is a democracy, where people's voices are heard!

It's a scary world to live in where kids are nervous to go to school because their parents support a particular political party, and it's not okay that my mom's book club was canceled because another mother refused to let people into her home who voted for a candidate she detested. So many vicious arguments are sparked by an initial miscommunication, and by the time all parties have calmed down they remember they both actually just want the best for their country.

There has to be an end to all of this senseless hostility, and it starts with diplomacy. America needs to be able to handle disagreement with grace, and so does our president. In order for healing to begin, everybody needs to start biting their tongues, so that they can try to understand the other person's point of view, and where they are coming from. Like Atticus Finch put it: "You never really understand a person until you consider things from his point of view…until you climb into his skin and walk around in it." (To Kill A Mockingbird)

You're not changing anybody's mind by yelling and behaving disrespectfully. It doesn't mean we do away with debates either, but what we are trying to accomplish by them. The courtesy exercised by politicians engaged within them, is shamefully overdue for revision.

During the next four years, you have the power to start changing the tone of the conversation—don't waste it.

Best of Luck,
Joanna Shepherd

# JONATHAN

## 17
## New Orleans, LA

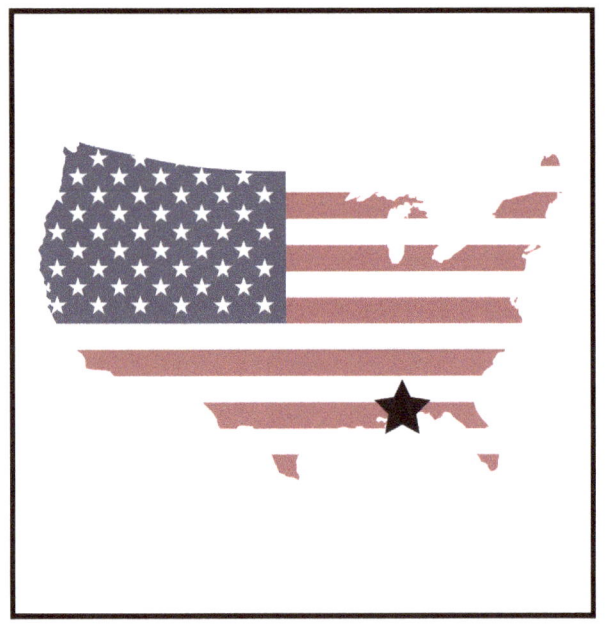

To Donald Trump,

You're not presidential material. You're a model of all arrogant and stuck-up people.

A person who runs a country should be a leader for all, not someone who insults. You cannot be trusted, because your actions affect everybody in the whole United States.

A president should be somebody who cares about everyone achieving success. You only think for yourself.

Think of yourself as just a citizen who wants to be treated equal.

Jonathan

# MARLOWE BARRINGTON

### 15
### Seattle, WA

## Take It To The Streets!

Rain streamed through gutters and splashed at our heels as we rushed across the street, nearing Westlake Park. My dad and I had decided to join a vigil after the deaths of Alton Sterling and Philando Castile. Both men had been murdered by the police within a span of two days.

Despite the weather, a large crowd had gathered, and in the center a man stood tall, megaphone in hand.

"Whose lives matter?" He shouted.

"Black lives matter!" The crowd said back in a chorus of overlapping voices.

"I said whose lives matter?"

"Black lives matter!" The crowd roared, and he nodded before he began to speak passionately. His voice was barely audible despite the megaphone in his hand. He spoke of his brother, who just a few months ago had been shot by the Seattle Police Department. A hush fell over us. He told us that he had a plan to help make a change to police departments everywhere. Though I only caught every few things he said, it became clear to me that those who could didn't agree with him.

A woman in the crowd shouted her protest. I heard cries of 'let her speak' which went unanswered, as the man pushed forward in his speech. This woman refused to be ignored. She finally got a hold of a megaphone and her sharp voice rang out: "This law won't change a thing! We've seen it time and time again and we know our voices will not be heard. Take it to the streets!"

"You're crazy," one lady said.

"Just let him finish!"complained another. Yet somehow, one by one, she got us all to stand up and abandon the concrete park where we'd gathered.

"Take it to the streets!" a voice shouted. And so we did. We marched through downtown, traffic halting in our wake. I felt strong then, empowered. Like we were taller than the gray office buildings that towered on either side of us.

"No justice! No peace! No racist police!" The cheers of onlookers fueled us on. Our parade grew until we stretched for streets long. Police on bicycles stopped the traffic. People photographed and videoed our procession. We were invincible, until we weren't.

We had stopped at a stoplight in front of the highway. In the center of the group, the woman who had brought us here encouraged others to speak up. To voice their stories, their ideas. A helicopter whizzed overhead. For the first time, I noticed that the police who had been guiding the traffic were now gathered behind us. A line of white allies in the group formed a barrier between protesters and police, to protect those without their privilege. We stood for what felt like an hour, just listening. People shifted from one foot to the other, a restlessness that manifested in two ways: leave or do something drastic.

"We need to take the highway!" a man hollered over the muttering in the crowd. "Yeah! Take the highway!"

As people edged towards the tunnel, the police shifted, blocking our path. It became clear to us then that we had to act immediately, or our efforts would be in vain. I took my dad's hand and we ran up the hill, towards the highway exit.

"Hurry!" people shouted, and we surged forward.

The police made it first, forming a barricade with their bikes in front of them. We ran to the other side instead. Just like before, the policemen who had before seemed like they were helping us blocked our path. A shot pierced the air.

Around me people screamed and ducked. Many ran away. The shot I heard was not a gun, only a small firecracker-like ball meant to scare us. Still, I felt rattled to my core. A man, not a few yards ahead of me, approached the bikes. A policeman sprayed him with pepper spray and he cried out in pain. Voices of indignation rose. Finally, my dad pulled me back. Two more men were sprayed in the commotion.

"I can't let you get hurt," my dad told me firmly. I could tell he was scared for me.

We never did make it onto the highway. On the local news that night I saw a story about our protest. It told me that the man who'd been pepper sprayed had run aggressively towards the police, that another had shouted obscenities at them. It angered me that the media, who had ignored the murders of Alton Sterling and Philando Castile, also twisted our story. We had been peaceful, but that wasn't what they said. This was another example of the voices of marginalized people not being heard. I had heard about this but never witnessed it before. I felt good about going to the protest and for standing for what I believe in, but knowing that in a few weeks our efforts would be forgotten made me feel hopeless.

People like to think that racism only manifests itself when people interact, but it goes far beyond that. It manifests itself in how our country operates—from education, to the media, to law enforcement. I tell you about this experience so you don't forget. If you're not outraged, you're in denial. I challenge you to take action.

# McKinley Gough

**15**
Taylorsville, UT

Dear Mr. President,

I do not know what a president does for family time. A vacation doesn't seem reasonable, especially since you now run a country. But one thing I think every family does in their free time is play board games. Board games teach us much about life: Clue teaches us deduction, Monopoly teaches us how to amass money, and Risk teaches us when to attack. I have heard your critics (namely my dad) say that you will destroy public relations with foreign countries. I have more faith in you than that, but I don't want you to do something like that on purpose because war is Risk, not Monopoly.

One of your main campaign themes was your insistence that you are not a politician, but a businessman. I firmly believe that you would destroy me in a game of Monopoly. You are now in charge of the most influential army in the world, but when it comes to war forget your Monopoly skills. Wars can occasionally improve the economy, create new weapons that can become great amenities like the microwave, but it also can destroy the economy. Remember that the Great Depression drove out the Trump family from Germany and gave rise to three totalitarian leaders. Despite the potential economic gain, do NOT treat another country like Boardwalk and drop a big American house on it.

I am a fairly good Risk player. All I have to do is capture Australia early in a game and it's a free win. Knowing when to fight, and when not to is now a daily decision for you. If you honestly think that deploying the army into a full on war would be the best move for America and its people, I have to trust you. You are now our president and I sincerely hope that we elected a man who is good at Risk.

Board games all have rules. It's the only thing that makes them fun. If some one said "move your piece around a board," no one would care. If someone said "move your piece around a board and try and solve a murder," then people will and do love it. War is a tricky thing. There are rules to war, not that the United States sanctions any of them. There are no Get Out of Jail Free cards. You can't turn in three cards and get more troops. When it comes to war, you as our president have to be careful.

Everyone knows about war. It has always been seen in a positive light. It makes popular video games and cool movies, but it is not a good thing. The very first book about how awful war is was "All Quiet on the Western Front" by Erich Maria Remarque. It's not a new thing, but please keep in mind that it should never be for economic gain, that it is a game of Risk.

Wishing you luck in the leadership of our country.

Sincerely,
McKinley Gough

# Jillian Jackson

### 15
### Sammamish, WA

## Melting Pot Mother Tongue

Dear Donald Trump,

You seem to speak in your own language,
an ancient dialect of discrimination.
It is a language that marks women as
your ornaments, accessories, and conquests.
It is a language that labels minorities
in one-dimensional stigmas.
It is a language that proclaims that marriage
is not an unalienable right for all.
Some of us speak a tongue of tolerance.
Can we teach you?

We agree "women belong in the House,
the Senate, and in protecting
the sanctity of our own bodies."
We are all temples of formidable rock,
ornate but never merely ornamental.
Our columns are not for you to chip at,
our doors not for you to enter without asking.
The voices emanating from us may be soft
or clanging of Clinton steel.
But no temple is "nasty."

## - Dear Mr. President -

We declare that "Black Lives Matter,"
unapologetically affirming self-worth
of somebody you see synonymous
with the name tag of Inner City Born.
I will not let you label them,
in a thick Sharpie too quick to judge
and too permanent to erase.
Identifies are sometimes composed of color,
sometimes of gender, sometimes of orientation,
but they are not yours to write.

We sing "Love is Love",
and though our voices crack with
hate crimes committed at night clubs,
we keep our hymns playing.
The tentative strings of tolerance and
the overwhelming orchestra of acceptance
grow in American voices.
And even if you cut our vocal chords
in the form of Supreme Court reversals,
we will still be louder than you.

We speak so many languages.
Spanish "r"s roll off some tongues,

others elongate the "a"s in the Arabic alphabet.
You remain in your linguistic imperialism,
labeling those who struggle with English as broken.
But language does not snap off like a bone,
it morphs and twists like a muscle.
These are our temples, our declarations, our songs.

This is our melting pot mother tongue.
I hope you become more fluent.

# Emma Fryer

### 17
### West Jordan, UT

Dear President Trump,

My name is Emma Fryer. I am seventeen years old. I live in West Jordan, Utah and I could not vote in the election, but the youth of America are the voices of the future and they deserve to be heard.

I will remember your election day with great vividness. I went to bed at 12:00 a.m. You needed six votes more and in a surreal—possibly naive—daze, I headed to bed confident that in the morning I would wake to Hillary Clinton's acceptance speech. That is not what happened. I woke up to the news I never thought I would hear. I read the articles in disbelief as I left for the day, still having not fully processed the news.

I turned on my car and immediately the radio declared "...President Elect Trump." I screamed "I can't do it!" and flicked the dial to the left. I drove silently to school with tears on my face and ended up in the classroom of one of my favorite teachers. I explained how I felt—that there was so much value in being on the right side of history, and I wanted that for my country.

We cried, but then the bell rang. We wiped our tears, and I walked out of her class with my head high, ready to fight for the next four years and beyond for what I know is right. This, I believe, is the story of many. This is our fight.

I would be lying if I said I wasn't scared. However, I know now that the true strength of America is in the people who continue to fight for what they believe in when the odds are stacked against them. I was eight years old when president Obama was elected. I remember even then realizing how important his election was to our country; to every African American past, present and future; to all minorities. This however, has also meant I never feared that the values I held wouldn't be reflected in the presidential administration.

The fear that I have now is foreign to me, but it is making me stronger every day. It makes me want to fight harder, to continue working each day for the America I know is possible. One in which differences are celebrated, and no one fears for their safety on grounds of race, gender or sexual orientation. One in which everyone has the opportunity to live a life they are proud of.

Mr. President, I am not hoping for you to fail, for that goes against the interests of our entire country. What I am hoping for now is a change of heart. I hope you realize that the diversity of our nation is what makes it exceptional. The coming together of many cultures, languages, walks of life, and religions has shaped our country for its entire history.

I hope you learn that climate change is not a hoax, and that it is a threat to all of life on our Earth and that the future of our planet is no partisan issue. I hope you learn that The Affordable Care act is essential to the well being of millions of Americans, and that repeal would be detrimental to many.

I hope you'll understand that Mexican immigrants are not rapists and drug dealers, that refugees are not "poisoned Skittles."

These are humans who are looking to America—the nation that has the words "Give me your tired, your poor, your huddled masses" inscribed on the statue that has greeted refugees for over a century—to honor their promise to the world.

I also hope you realize that women are infinitely important to the advancement of our country; that when we hold half of our population back, we are inhibiting the progress of our entire world. I want my country to represent one in which women are respected, appreciated, and understood.

I hope you realize that America is great. It is "beautiful, trail blazing, unique, young, teaching, learning" great. America still has a lot of work to do, but I have never doubted its greatness. I hope you are able to take pride in the nation you have been given the honor of representing internationally.

Mr. Trump, I am willing you to try your best to bridge the rift in our country this earthquake of an election has created. I urge you to show Americans that we are all more alike than we are different, and that when we are united, there is nothing we cannot do. I hope you will listen to the people of our nation. All the people of our nation. Listen to what they say, because they want change and they see that in you.

Finally, the next four years are full of uncertainty for me. But I know that all the Americans who are reeling right now will persevere. I know that our country is going to continue to be full of diverse people, viewpoints, cultures, faiths and more. These are and will continue to be the greatest thing about our great nation.

I am hopeful, I am scared, I am proud, I am hurt, I am invigorated.

Dear Mr. President America, is watching.

Emma Fryer

# Emily Edwards
### 17
### Lee's Summit, MO

Dear President Trump,

I suppose the best way to begin this letter is by introducing myself. My name is Emily Dawn Edwards. I am a sophomore in the 'Show Me State' and seventeen years old. I spent the last year dedicating myself to the Air Force Junior Reserve Officer Training Corps, where I currently hold an officer's position. In the same time, I have quite frankly hoped you would not become president.

I have feared to serve under you in the U.S. Army, beginning the summer of 2019. That being said, I have a few words to say to you.

I am not thrilled that you will be my president though I will not protest; you have won fairly. While I was not a fan of former Secretary of State Hillary Clinton either, I found her more qualified. She is poised and professional. Mrs. Clinton also never made references to her genitals. However, none of this proves that you will be a bad president.

I hope during your time at The Oval Office you consider this: The people of the United States deserve to be heard—including those of us under eighteen. Before you make promises you can't keep, think of those who are counting on them. Be prideful in your position, not boastful; it was given to help our nation and not to shame it.

A good thing for you to focus on is to repair all the foreign allies you have alienated. Treat women with respect and not with derogatory catcalls. Discourage your followers against the violence and harm of those who do not share the same religious views, heritage, skin color, or country.

Please consider everything stated in this letter and every other entry written in this book as you step into the White House this January. Remember, you no longer represent just yourself but rather our entire country.

Sincerely,
Emily Edwards

# DESHAWN

17
New Orleans, LA

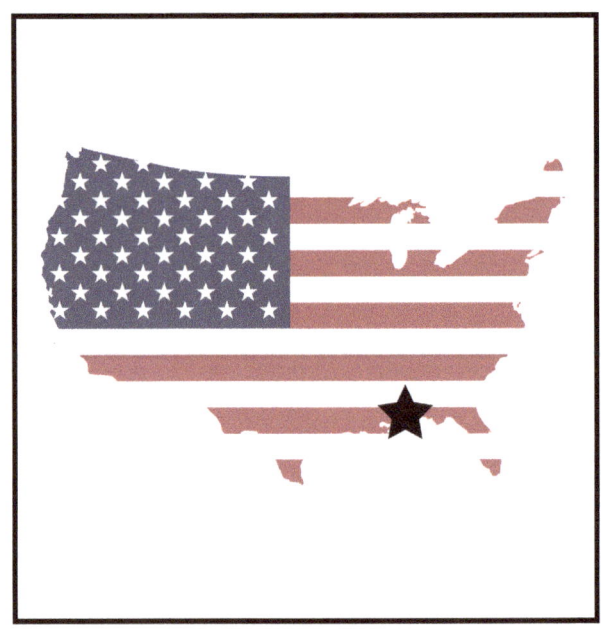

Dear Mr, President,

I really don't know you, and I would like to meet you. I would like to talk about our struggles throughout the community of New Orleans.

Since you're the POTUS now, you should be respected as a man. You should also treat America like your family—not just take care of the rich and forget the poor.

Make America great again the right and civil way. Let's make America great again the strong, stand-together way.

Deshawn

# RILEY

## 15
### Pittsburgh, PA

Dear Mr. President,

What am I to you? To my friends, I'm a lighthearted jokester who has quips for everyone and is ready to debate the topic of the day at a moment's notice. To my school, I am an honor roll student. To my country, I am a free man, one whose possibilities should be endless. And yet, this election has split my friends, my school, and my country, and for what?

I still recall seeing that another student had written your name in chalk right in front of the school; it nearly made me puke. I live a privileged life, which is why it hit me so hard when I saw how other people were struggling; it made me want to go out and give them a hand, to help in their times of need. I can never truly understand the pain that African Americans, Muslims, women, and other minorities go through, but that won't stop me from wanting to help them. What about you?

Many claim that you can make America great again, but I want to know what makes America "great." I'll tell you what makes America great: the fact that it is a country for everyone. We learned that Ronald Reagan once told Mikhail Gorbachev to "Tear down this wall," while he spoke about the barrier between East and West Berlin. Well, when it comes to the wall of racism, sexism, and homophobia, we need to tear down this wall, not continue building it.

We spend too much being upset with one another and not

enough time being kind. This scares me; it scares my family, my friends, my community, and a huge portion of my country. My vision of a great country is not a "great" country—it's an accepting country. It's not about excluding anyone; it's about including everyone, something we don't do enough of! I'm usually the happiest guy around, but it's hard to smile when it comes to the issues we face with discrimination, and I don't see how it will be better under your leadership.

While I cannot directly relate to racism or sexism, I can with homophobia. I live in a school where the word "faggot" is tossed around like a goddamn hacky sack, and as someone whose life has been enveloped in the LGBTQ community, I can say that I want to smash a table every time I hear it. You can help make this a nation of people who no longer have to feel the pain of being discriminated against or made fun of. I don't think you realize how hard it is to try and speak out against these actions; I've been made fun of, taunted, and laughed at for being someone who believes in political correctness, something you personally disapprove of. I fear that the message is that being gay, bisexual, transgender, or any other sexuality makes you different. I want the ability to go to the prom with a fellow male and not have all eyes on me. I knew the risk of coming out as someone who is interested in both men and women; I was well aware. I know I might sound selfish in acting as though I myself am being attacked when my pain cannot compare to what others have felt, but when my community and my beliefs are attacked and considered "not normal," I do feel pain. I hope that I can see the day where there is no reason to treat people differently because of who they are. Instead, we celebrate our diversity as a country as a point of pride.

Speaking of dreams, I have a good grasp on mine. I dream of an America where we stop caring about who is in the minority, and care more about what we work towards together. I dream of an America where all voices are heard, not just to show us different perspectives, but also as a sign of respect. I dream not of an America of whites, not of an America of blacks, not of an America of this religion or that religion; I dream of an America for all. I dream that the word "discrimination" becomes lost in the past and is never uttered in any city of any state. And I dream of not feeling "different" because of who I am. I sometimes think that these dreams are pointless, often staying up at night as I contemplate what I can do to achieve them. It all leads back to one major thing: the people of this country working together.

I do hope that you reconsider your current plan for your presidency, which appears to be ignoring the wishes of minorities and only focusing on yourself. I understand that you think you mean only the best, but you seem clueless on what "the best" is. You cannot make America great again because America is still great, and you cannot change that. I want to be able to live in a country where I feel both safe and free. And I know that I'm not the only one who feels a bit scared that I'm not going to be safe and fee in the future.

I'm tired of division; I'm tired of the arguments. I just want my friends and family to come together as one again. That's it.

It is impossible to see how the future of our country will turn out; it all depends on the path we take. Mr. President, take us down the right path—the path of truth and justice; the path of love, not war; the path of the people. Mr. President, take us down the path of America. That, perhaps, is my one true wish.

Don't let me down.

Sincerely,
Riley

# Rebecca Fields

15
New York City, NY

Dear President Trump,

I am afraid for the future of this country. I am afraid that bigotry, racism, sexism, misogyny, and sexual assault will become normal. I am afraid that the power of the President will be abused. I am afraid that energy will be cultivated in ways that result in more hatred.

I am afraid that I will no longer have control over my own body. I am afraid that if I am sexually assaulted, what actually happened will be questioned because of how attractive someone else thinks I am. I am afraid to go to college out of fear that I will be sexually assaulted and nothing will happen.

I am afraid that I will not be able to stand up for what I believe in. I am afraid that when I stand up, I will be pushed down harder.

I am afraid that my friends and family, and everyone I love will be threatened by this new holder of power. I am afraid that the values of our new president will have an impact on the way the people in this country think. I am afraid that the way our new president thinks will become the new and normal way of thinking.

I am afraid that four years will turn into eight years. I am afraid that getting back the progress over the next four years that we have gained over the past eight years will turn into an eight-year fight.

My left fist is fighting against hatred. My right fist is fighting for rights. My body is a barrier that will not be broken or abused. My body is a barrier that is strong for keeping Trump out as the wall he promises to build

    I know that fighting for what I and everyone believes in will be a never-ending fight; I know we will be fighting until the day we die For what we want. For the rights we believe in.

Rebecca Fields

# CECE JANE

18
Los Angeles, CA

Dear Mr. President,

I am a high school senior from Los Angeles, California, and I will be going to university next year. Hence, I am on the precipice of entering the adult world where I will take part in shaping the future of our nation and our planet, as it is my generation that will one day inherit these responsibilities.

For me, the United States represents freedom for all, and a land that is a refuge for mankind. We were founded on these very principles. I often think of how lucky I am to have been born in America.

Here is a snapshot of my story.

During the election, I lost a lot of friends. As the weeks wore on, I felt surrounded by a growing culture of my peers that included bigotry, hatred, misogyny, and xenophobia. It was as if my peers felt empowered to boast of their prejudices. I have been a part of a group of girls during high school, but suddenly I realized that my ideology clashed with them. One "friend" told me that she would "own a slave." This is coming from a girl who is dating a black man. This comment sincerely upset me and thus ended our friendship.

Another told me that her best friend from Iran (legally living in America) "does not have a right to live in America because she was not born here." Another told me that my beautiful, sweet, kind, childhood babysitter is a "bad Mexican." Then came the talk about the Syrians. "Keep them out," they all said, including my friend who was born in India but lives in America legally. "They will take our jobs."

These statements come from people who hardly attend school to gain a skill set to get a job. They all just turned their cheek to the war and devastation others were experiencing, only to protect their own presumed interests. And so, as the days went by, I found myself more and more wondering, "who are these young Americans, those that will graduate with me come June? And, why do they see the world from such a contrasting vantage point than I?"

First I thought, "It is Mr. Trump who is giving them permission to hate, to be bigots, misogynists and xenophobes." But as I thought about it more, I realized that one man could not possibly have created this mindset alone. And I realized that the most important thing that I could do in the next four years while I am in college is to work toward promoting education for all. Because I realized it is a lack of education that has made everyone full of fear and hate. They simply do not understand, and somehow, we as a nation have not given them the tools to understand that intolerance is abhorrent.

And so, my vision is that my peers all have the opportunity to learn, to become educated. I implore you, Mr. President, to prioritize an educational initiative that will "Make American Education Great." Teach the youth to think, not to fear; to undertake critical analysis, not to hate. For we cannot live in a world where we hate and fear each other. The future must instead include a world where we are inclusive and we love each other.

Sir, you have four years to be a role model to the youth, to kids like me across America, and I implore you to be a role model that teaches tolerance and inclusion. Be a leader that will go down in history as a humanitarian—someone who evolved the thinking of mankind, who gave kids the tools to think and learn.

This, Mr. President, is my vision for your presidency.

With deep respect,
Cece Jane

# Margaret Rose Marie Higgins
## 17
### Edmonds, WA

Dear Mr. President and Mr. Vice President,

Before now, I have never been genuinely afraid to live in America.

I'm scared both as a woman and as a member of the LGBTQA community. Your positions, as well as those of your supporters, frighten me. You both are open supporters of conversion therapy. To be honest, I wasn't aware that we have reverted back to the nineteenth century. I had thought that we as a nation, as well as us as a world, had come further than this.

Saying that people aren't good enough the way they are, or that they need to change in order to be accepted, is part of why we have such a high suicide rate.

I thought that we were to the point where people who need to get help can, without facing the ridicule of an ignorant nation; and that those who are perfectly fine the way they are, aren't constantly told that they need to change.

I simply do not understand anymore. Yet again, we have devolved.

Sincerely afraid,
Margaret Rose Marie Higgins

# Sophia Gruber

### 16
### West Hartford, CT

Dear Mr. President,

I am going to begin by saying that although I am writing this in the format of a letter to President Donald Trump, I will be speaking to my fellow Americans overall.

I am sixteen years old and I've decided to write this letter today to make my voice heard. I understand that I am not old enough to make my vote count. I may not even be old enough to make a difference, however, I am old enough to have my own opinion.

I live in the "true blue" state of Connecticut, which means that for the most part, we are a democratic state. Although I live in a democratic state, there are many people here that value conservative republican beliefs.

I've been exposed to both sides of the political spectrum in my lifetime, and I believe that it shouldn't matter where someone stands politically. We are one nation and we need to start acting like it. In my opinion, this election has been one of the most interesting elections we've ever had—definitely in my lifetime. Any feelings regarding the election results are completely understandable. Whether it's fear, anger, disappointment, confusion or excitement; any feeling is valid. Everyone is entitled to their own opinion. However, when it reaches the point where someone makes an inappropriate comment about a specific race, ethnicity or gender, that's when it's been taken too far.

Many people agree with the ideas that President Trump has

proposed, but certain ideas he has have seriously offended so many others. I'm not here to belittle anyone's opinions on what's right or what's wrong, but I do believe that every human being in the world should be treated as such. In President Barack Obama's victory speech, he stated that "It doesn't matter whether you're black or white or Hispanic or Asian or Native American, or young or old, or rich or poor, abled or disabled, gay or straight. You can make it here in America if you're willing to try. I believe we can seize this future together because we are not as divided as our politics suggest."

I agree wholeheartedly with this statement. I believe that every person should be treated equally regardless of their skin color, ethnicity, sexuality or gender. Everyone is different in some way and instead of trying to change that, we should be proud of the diversity of this country. Since this election, fear has been a very relevant feeling from people who come from backgrounds that President Trump has spoken negatively about.

I am not writing this letter to attack President Trump or to give my opinions on the new President. I am simply stating how people are feeling about his election. President Trump has made it clear that he wants us to come together as one nation, and I agree with that idea and believe we have what it takes to get there. However, we will become one nation if, and only if, we all accept each other and respect each other equally.

Equal rights for women has been a prevalent issue for decades and it has dramatically evolved over time, with women's right to vote and to keep the same jobs as men. Women have been fighting and will keep fighting for total equality until this goal is met. President Donald Trump has made several extremely degrading remarks about women and although I do understand that every American is entitled to say what they think is true, I think that as a leader, President Trump could have avoided speaking this poorly of women. It is alarming that the man we now call our leader has spoken so offensively about half of the American population.

America is a united nation made up of people from all backgrounds, with all kinds of beliefs. This diversity is what makes us such a successful country, and it's what makes us proud to live here. The progress we've made in the past decade has been a tremendous achievement for America. There's no doubt we have our flaws, but we can rise above them and make this country stronger by coming together to put an end to the unacceptable behaviors we've taken part in.

I hope that as President Trump takes his place in office, we will remain one nation, accepting all people, and knowing that our diversity makes us a stronger country.

Thank you,
Sophia Gruber

# Erin Blake

**16**
**Salt Lake City, UT**

Hear Ye, Hear Ye all Past, Pres"id"ent, & Future,

I believe in freedom. I believe it was meant to be and should be the foundation we the people stand on.

But you, Mr. Trump—your opinions go against everything I stand for. I want to give voice to those without one, but now you want to take away my voice.

People feel threatened by your voice. People all over the world are scared for their lives. And honestly, I think that should be raising some serious red flags.

I cannot believe that every other sentence out of your mouth during the election was bigoted or racist or misogynistic, and that people liked it! People actually voted for someone willing to take away basic human rights.

I thought we were progressing as a nation, but now here you are, ready and willing to drop us back into the dark ages when there was a beheading every other Tuesday.

And your VP? He might be even worse than you.

I will never accept you as my president. You couldn't be trusted with your Twitter at the end of the election. How can we trust you with the nuclear launch codes?

I understand that some who read this letter will take offense to it. "It's an outrage!" they'll say. "It's his right as an American to say what he wants! Free speech!"

Well, to those people, I say this: According to the clause of the

Supreme Court case Schenck v. the U.S., free speech will not be protected if there is a 'clear and present danger'.

I'm pretty sure all those threats you made, 'Mr. President', fall under that category.

In truth, I didn't really like any of the candidates. All have something to say, but none of them actually know what it is they're saying. No doubt they don't even write their own speeches.

According to the statistics I've seen, Hillary won the popular vote, yet that and countless calls for a recount are ignored. It's given to us like we hold some choice in the matter of who will lead us; but current events claim the opposite.

Freedom is becoming a beautiful illusion. We are given two choices, unaware that if we were to look a little farther, we'd see a third choice—not a change of leadership, but a change of system.

The current system is rigged—not in our favor, or Trump's, or Hillary's, but in the favor of those truly in power. They are running the game behind the curtain, making the rises and falls in our economy, keeping us in line. And though we cry out for change and salvation, our voices continue to go unheard.

For the people, by the people. Not anymore.

Truly un-yours,
Erin Blake

# Sierra Wilson-Bailey

## 17
## Los Angeles, CA

## Living In Fear

The 2016 election brought out a lot of emotions from across the country. This election is the first one that I can actually understand.

The president of the United States is just talking folderol. I feel like he says certain things just to get a rise out of people. I just don't understand how he won.

This election is just ineffable for me. It broke my heart to see the minorities cry out because they don't know what their future holds. Everybody keeps saying to "have faith" or to "come together". But how can we when the majority of the people elected a man who isn't a pundit in politics? Racism is just going to be out there more, even though it has never gone away.

As a young woman of color, I have fear in my heart. I just wonder, "Am I going to be okay if I go to college in the South?' To see people cry and protest about an election is heartbreaking. Many people aren't even safe in their own country. Many want to leave.

How do we move forward? Is there going to be a war next? Are our people going to have jobs, welfare or health insurance? These are the questions that make me wonder if we are actually going to be okay as a country.

I just hope that the people who are in the office with Mr. Trump teach and mold him into a great president. If they can do this, I pray that we won't live in fear while he is in office for the next four years.

# Annie Braun

## 12
## New York City, NY

Dear President Donald J. Trump,

Congratulations! You put a lot of thought, care, and time into winning the 2016 presidential election. Did it sink in yet that you won? America chose you!

I woke up today hoping that it was all a dream. My mom woke me up early on election day to go vote with her. Why? Because she wanted to be with her daughter the day the first female President was elected.

As you may know, New York City had a sad, rainy day. I will have to learn to look up to you and respect you as President, or at least fake it.

President Trump, I am a twelve year old girl growing into a young woman and I want to feel as equal as men. I hope you can help. You say you have respect for women. Do they have respect for you? You speak your mind, something we all want to be able to do. I know you enjoy the right to do that. My older brother is gay and my younger brother is Hispanic, I'm scared that they won't have the right to do that.

I don't want you to stop fighting for what you believe in. Try and win New York's vote even if the elections are over. Never stop trying as hard as you have been. Do I feel safe with you as the president? The answer is 'no', but trust me: if you really tried harder, than I think that I could. I hate when people in my grade talk about you or how Hillary Clinton should have won. There is nothing we can do now. I hope people can move on. I'll try.

It will take me more than a letter to tell you what I have to say. I would love to meet you and see the good in you—the good you had before the election, when you were friends with the Clintons and were not accused of sexual harassment of women.

I know you may be thinking that I am only twelve. I'm not, I'm more than just a number and a name. I support the people who need it the most. The people who were affected by you. I'm excited. Excited to read the news and see the good and bad our country has to offer. We need a balance. Our country is not split, but balanced. We have opinions from the people hidden in shadows: the gun owners, the poor, the rich, the evil, the good.

I'm a writer, a photographer, a student at a Jewish private school, and an LGBTQ supporter. I was a Hillary supporter. I will be a young woman under your presidency. My Bat Mitzvah is coming up. I will technically be a woman to my peers. I hope I am not treated like a woman who encounters you.

I hope that as you take the White House I can encounter you and tell my friends: "I met Donald Trump, supporter of all, leader of the nation, selfless human, and great public speaker who changed our generation with every word for the better."

When I can say that, let me know. Let me tell you in person how I feel. Let me know when you think that I will be happy—when the disabled, teen mothers, women, LGBTQ community, people of color, and our country will be able to all say at once, "That Donald

Trump, I'm glad he won. He made a difference, a difference we needed."

    Let's make America Great Again? When was it ever this good? Thank you for reading this letter. It means so much to me.

Sincerely,
Annie Braun

P.S. Will there be a war? What does it feel like to be President? Will you listen?

# Kara Batson

### 17
### Los Angeles

## My Dream for America

I long to live in an America which embraces challenges
as they come along,
and a brotherhood of man
as we sing our national song.

I long for a nation of innovators
who actively seek solutions,
and leaders who listen to their people,
while following the Constitution.

I long for a bond
between the commoners and leaders
instead of a huge gap
between the speakers and the readers.

I long for a democracy
where every person has a say,
and where there are plenty of options
for all citizens to weigh.

But most of all I long for a home
where I can have a voice—
a place where I can go outside
and feel like I have a choice.

# Kinsey Makkar

16
Los Angeles, CA

Mr. Trump,

In my household, you were known as the funny, well-to-do business-guy who had his own show and coined the phrase "You're fired!" And that's just about all we knew of you.

But, as I began to know more and more about you, I grew fearful. As I learned that you were soon to become our president, I became immensely afraid for my life, and other minorities around me, and I'll tell you why.

## ON PEOPLE OF COLOR (POC)

Growing up in such a liberal country where everyone is known for being special and unique in their own way, it is still always hard to make yourself be known. Being a person of color (POC) has always been something I have learned to embrace, and embrace to the fullest. I knew, that in learning to love my skin tone and in learning my unique attributes, I would be unstoppable… until I learned about racism.

When the unlawful shooting of Trayvon Martin occurred in 2012, I was eleven years old. That's when my awareness of the racial divide in this country really hit me. Does your son, at almost eleven years old, ever have to feel this way?

It hit me, honestly, like a ton of bricks, knowing that it could have been my brother, or any family member of mine shot dead in the street just because he was wearing black skin and a hoodie—which made him "suspicious," according to George Zimmerman. It's as if the weather doesn't range from 49-54 degrees at night in Florida in February, as if wearing a hoodie over one's head is a threat, as if wearing a hoodie over one's head is illegal.

As this culture of perpetual racial profiling shootings have continued, where have you been, Mr. Next President? Where have you been to stand up and represent the POC and take action to implement change for the sake of us?

As I've scrolled and scrolled away to find statistics and numbers to prove that police brutality shootings were primarily inflicted upon African Americans or people of color, I decided to draw back. You're an incredibly capable man who, just as well as I, can search the Internet and see the countless number of men and women whose faces pop up with the click of a button as victims—victims such as Tamir Rice, Ezell Ford, Michael Brown and many others. It's quite depressing.

## ON IMMIGRATION

In America, a place founded on immigration, I was appalled to learn that one of your goals was to "build a wall" and kick the immigrants out—back to Mexico—and make them pay for it. As a reminder, in U.S. History class 101, we learned that the early white colonial settlers raped, pillaged, and stole what rightfully belonged to the Native Americans. So, when speaking on the sensitive topic of immigration, we need to be clear about who we call the "rapists" and "killers." How about we call the Mexican immigrants "undocumented, hardworking families that would gladly pay taxes and benefit from representation" as we allow them to become a proud part of our society?

Just because a small ratio of undocumented Mexicans may have caused illegal harm, it doesn't make it okay to keep the rest of them out for wanting to acquire a space for their families in the "Land of Opportunity". So, I ask, how can we kick people out because they don't have citizenship? Why is it "illegal" to want to live in the country you so-call "great"? Who has the right to force these established, hard-working families out (who, contrary to your opinion, are not rapists or killers), for the sole reason of being undocumented?

The next time immigration is brought up, I hope you remember where the root of it began in America.

## ON WOMEN

"No one respects women more than I do." –Donald Trump on CNN with interviewer Wolf Blitzer.

*Really? Does the man, who isn't pro-choice, really think he respects women the most?* My answer is "no." How can it be claimed that you respect or represent a group, when you and the "anti-pro choice camp" will blindly make a decision for them? Can't you see masses of women beg for the choice to have the right to decide what they would like to do with their own bodies? The better question is, "Why do women have to beg men in politics to request respect and permission for what they'd find best for themselves?" The answer that American politicians, such as yourself and your cabinet, should come to agree upon is: "They don't." Men cannot fathom what it's like to be a woman, or know how burdensome a pregnancy can be for people who cannot afford to maintain a healthy lifestyle for themselves and a child. This is one of many policies of yours that I'm unclear on.

"Just in case I start kissing her"... and "grab them by the pussy." This is what you called "locker room banter," right? Well, whether it was "locker room banter" or your true thoughts, your words have exalted a rape-culture whether you believe it or not.

If you respect women, do you greet them by grabbing their genitalia? Last I looked, that's how dogs greet each other. I understand that your rebuttal is that this occurred eleven years ago; however, a dog eleven years ago is still a dog today.

I hope and pray that your purposed evolution is in favor of the 157 million women that you will soon represent, commencing on your inauguration day.

Most children grow up learning that your genitals are your NO-NO area. Knowing that my president is okay with grabbing women's NO-NO areas, on any scale, is scary. Being the leader of the "free world," you set precedence for how other men will behave. After all, the Presidency of the United States of America is among the most desired and regarded position any American can hold.

And lastly, just so you know, many women are scared and terrified that their next president has stamped "approved" on the continuation of such obscene, lewd and repulsive behavior. It's disgusting and concerning.

Mr. Trump, the overarching goal and purpose of this letter is to exercise my first amendment right and communicate my heartfelt concerns as a U.S. citizen. Because you are our next president, mine and other people's futures are in your hands. I ask that you please acknowledge every minority group and help lead them in ways that will be beneficial for generations to come. I trust that you will not take this job too lightly.

Without further ado, I truly do wish you the best of luck during your presidency, and I pray that the "God we trust" (stated on the American currency you so adore), is the God you will consult when leading our country to victory.

America wishes you luck.

With sincerest regards,
Kinsey Makkar

# SOPHIE DOWNING

### 17
### Seattle, WA

## Speaking Out

While babysitting on the night of the election, I continually refreshed the polls on my phone in-between the stories I read to the third grader beside me.

Before her parents left, her mom knelt down beside her and promised to wake her up to celebrate the historical election we were sure was going to happen that night. But, as the time ticked by and more and more states finalized their votes, the realization occurred to me that maybe the election would not turn out as I had hoped.

After trading somber goodbyes with the parents who had been so hopeful when they had left for the night, I got in my car and drove home in silence.

Later that night I cried—not because Mr. Trump himself had been elected to the highest office in the country, but more so because so many Americans shared his terrifying views regarding women, immigrants, and foreign relations. I also cried because I felt hopeless; that my voice and the voices of my peers would not be heard or taken into consideration regarding the election.

The next day, in my AP Government class, my usually loud and enthusiastic teacher was silent. When he finally spoke, he asked us to take out our journals and write about how we felt regarding the election: questions we may have, perspectives on the situation, or anything else that was on our mind. Since most of my classmates and I were seventeen at the time of the election, our voices weren't heard. And while I realized that Washington would continue to be a blue state without the measly votes of thirty Seattle teens, it still felt like we were part of the reason Secretary Clinton wasn't elected.

As the weeks have gone by, I have accepted the fact that Donald Trump will become our next President. But I will not accept that the things he supports will become normalized in our society, because if having values that are racist, sexist and xenophobic become the status quo, our country will have erased decades of progress that so many have fought for.

I also realize that I am extremely privileged, and that while I fear the impending repercussions for women after the outcome of this election, I am more worried for those who are not upper-middle-class, straight, non-practicing Christian white people who live in a liberal city. And while I do feel that I did not help Secretary Clinton's campaign, this election has inspired me to work harder and to fight for the rights and assumptions that I take for granted.

I hope that this election inspires more young people to fight for what they believe in and fight for the future they want. I also hope that the next time a president is elected, millions of citizens will not be afraid of the country that is supposed to be home to them.

# Yein Ji

**17**
**North Salt Lake, UT**

## A Message from Us

America is full of diversity
in every suburb and city.
My generation is the most diverse yet,
but we are not a threat.

Even though we are called the minority,
we are the majority.
We are the children of immigrants
and we will not be discriminant.

We know our skin color is not the same,
but that won't stop us; we will attain
the titles of doctors and teachers
entrepreneurs and preachers.

We won't be held down by stereotypes
or how you think we should act.
We are here for better lives
and we're not turning back.

# Acknowledgments

We want to extend a big thanks to all of the youth who took the time to put their thoughts, hopes, dreams and concerns on paper so their voices could be heard. These letters, poems and essays carry so much wisdom and power, and it is our hope that the people who govern our country—now and in the future—will listen to what they have to say.

I also want to offer a big thanks to Thea Chard, Juli Saeger Russell, Stephanie Durden Edwards, Corbin Lewars and Laurie Zettler—who all donated their time and incredible talents to make this project possible.

All proceeds from book sales will be donated to Rock the Vote, an organization dedicated to fostering youth involvement in politics.

If you would like to get involved and help ensure that projects such as these continue, please visit our program Web site: www.writeitoutloud.org.

Sincerely,
Ingrid Ricks
Founder, Write it Out Loud

www.ingramcontent.com/pod-product-compliance
Lightning Source LLC
Chambersburg PA
CBHW040324300426
44112CB00021B/2873